The Little Purple Book

By Common Consent Press is a nonprofit publisher dedicated to producing affordable, high-quality books that help define and shape the Latter-day Saint experience. BCC Press publishes books that address all aspects of Mormon life. Our mission includes finding manuscripts that will contribute to the lives of thoughtful Latter-day Saints, mentoring authors and nurturing projects to completion, and distributing important books to the Mormon audience at the lowest possible cost.

The Little Purple Book

MWEG Essentials

Mormon Women for
Ethical Government

BCC
PRESS

With gratitude for all the foremothers
and hope for all the daughters

The Little Purple Book: MWEG Essentials
Copyright © 2018 by Mormon Women for Ethical Government

For information contact
By Common Consent Press
4062 S. Evelyn Dr.
Salt Lake City, UT 84124-2250

Cover design: Tiffany Tertipes
Book design: Andrew Heiss

www.bccpress.org

ISBN-13: 978-1-948218-05-4
ISBN-10: 1-948218-05-4

10 9 8 7 6 5 4 3 2 1

Contents

MWEG: Our Vision and Mission

Mormon Women for Ethical Government (MWEG) is a nonpartisan group dedicated to the ideals of decency, honor, accountability, transparency, and justice in governing. We are faithful, peaceful, and proactive. We are both watchdogs and activists, guided by our discipleship to Jesus Christ and His teachings. Our goal is to oppose unethical proceedings and to promote positive change.

Members of this group are absolutely committed to civility and respectful discourse and conduct. We pledge to uphold the Six Principles of Peacemaking.[a] We will not engage in name-calling, vitriol, or hate speech of

---

a. See section IV, "Six Principles of Peacemaking."

any kind. We will seek to understand all sides of every issue before taking action.

Mormon Women for Ethical Government was born of desire, frustration, and hope: the desire to act, to push back with faith, love, and light against what we see as a tidal wave of corruption and self-interest in the political landscape; the frustration that comes from feeling directionless and alone in our efforts; and the hope that, working together, we can actually make a difference.

There is strength in numbers, power in organization.

We believe we were created to act and not to be acted upon. We know, too, that God expects us to be "anxiously engaged in a good cause, and do many things of [our] own free will, and bring to pass much righteousness; for the power is in [us]."[a]

These are strange times. We cannot stand by and do nothing. To do nothing is to be complicit.

And so we must act. But it is our belief that we must act always in kindness and with civility. A call for kindness and civility does not imply timidity or capitulation. It's simply a call for us to hearken to the better angels of our natures as we engage in the good fight.

In the words of Dr. Martin Luther King, Jr., "Darkness cannot drive out darkness; only light can do that. Hate cannot drive out hate; only love can do that."[b]

---

a. Doctrine and Covenants (D&C) 58:27–28

b. https://vimeo.com/24614519

And so, we will fight. We will fight with focus and determination and ferocity. We will drive out the darkness, drive out the hate—but with light, and with love, because those are the only weapons that can heal this broken world.

II

In the Beginning:
MWEG's Genesis Story

Sharlee Mullins Glenn, founder

It was kind of an accident—MWEG was. I had no idea when I opened up my computer on January 26, 2017, and created a Facebook group for a few close friends that I was setting in motion what would become a veritable movement, snowballing and gaining speed so quickly that we would all be left reeling.

But if it was an accident, it was a divine one—which means, of course, that it was no accident at all.

Just a few months earlier, after sending our last child (of five) off on his mission and then being released from the heavy stake calling that I had held for the past four and a half years, I had recommitted my life to my Heavenly Father and had pledged that I would do my best to do

4

whatever He asked of me, no matter how hard, or scary, or uncomfortable. "Use me," I said. "Let me be an instrument in thy hand."

There have been days, I must admit, when I have rued those words!

Like many Americans, I found myself growing increasingly alarmed in the months leading up to the 2016 presidential election. As the level of civility in our public discourse plummeted and the already gaping political divide in our nation widened, it seemed as though the very foundations of our democracy were beginning to crumble. I knew that I could not just sit by and do nothing.

What I didn't know was that that literally thousands of my sisters throughout the Church were feeling exactly the same way.

On January 25, 2017, I was engaged in an email exchange with my close friend since grad school, Melissa Dalton-Bradford. We were distraught by the deterioration of honor and decency that we were witnessing in the highest echelons of government. "What can we do?" we kept asking each other. Our response to that question was to become the foundation upon which MWEG would be built.

> What can we do? We must turn our dismay into action. But we can't panic. First, and above all, we seek the Spirit. We stay on our knees and pray our hearts out until we know

we have the Spirit with us. And then we get to work. Calmly, with focus, impelled by the ferocity of love, not fear, not anger. What do we do? We write and call every single one of our members of Congress, over and over again. We flood them with phone calls and letters and emails, and let them know that THIS MUST NOT STAND. And we use whatever other platforms are available to us to make our voices heard. We must work hard, but we also must work smart. Our power is greater the greater our numbers, so we have to mobilize.

We have to mobilize.

We carried our discussion over onto the private forum shared by the members of the board of *Segullah*, a literary journal/blog for Latter-day Saint women, where at some point I offered to set up a separate online group where we could continue to talk and strategize.

That evening, I sat down at my computer and created a Facebook group. I called it Mormon Women for Political Action, though we soon changed the name to Mormon Women for Ethical Government (MWEG). As I worked late into the night and into the wee hours of January 26 writing the group description and establishing the guidelines and core principles by which the group would be guided, I felt the unmistakable whisperings of the Spirit.

Once it was set up, I added the friends from *Segullah* who had indicated that they'd like to be part of this new discussion group. What I didn't do, and in hindsight wish I had, was ask people not to add anyone else to the group—at least not until we knew what we were doing.

Within 48 hours, we had 270 members. By day five, that number had grown to nearly 1,000. And within four weeks, we had over 4,000 members.

Clearly we had hit a nerve.

But now that 4,000 women had jumped aboard our little makeshift raft, it was time to sink or . . . build a seaworthy ship!

I'll let a few representative posts from the Facebook group help move the story forward:

January 28, 2017

Dear sisters in the cause, when I set up this page just a little over 48 hours ago, I had visions of a cozy little group of about 30. We have been overwhelmed by the response from all of you. As of now, we have over 270 members. It moves, encourages, and inspires me to think of what we can accomplish together by combining our voices, our abilities, our passion, our intellectual, physical, and spiritual resources.

January 31, 2017

Sisters, as of this moment, we are 920 strong, and there are 48 people in queue waiting to be approved. I find myself trembling at times, stunned by what has happened in the five days since I sat down at my computer after an impassioned and empowering discussion with my beautiful sisters on the Segullah board and started this group. As we approach 1,000 members, I feel your power and goodness like a literal force, thrumming and pulsating from my computer screen.

As Eliza R. Snow wrote after attending a special meeting of the Young Ladies' Mutual Improvement Association on September 26, 1877: "Those who are alive to their religion know that there is much to do. The sisters have weighty duties placed upon them, and duties that cannot be accomplished singly, but require a unity of heart and feeling. We must be united."

Thank you for being united in this cause. Thank you for flooding into this group and bringing with you so much energy and wisdom and intellect and integrity and power. There is much to be done, and together we will do it. Onward!

February 8, 2017

Again, we thank you all for your patience as we scramble to build the foundation necessary to support what we initially thought would be a modest little cottage where 25–30 of us could huddle together over cups of herbal tea brainstorming very specific plans for direct action but which has instead become a sprawling and mighty convention center teeming with beautiful, brave, strong women from all over the globe and all over the political spectrum, united by love, their devotion to the gospel of Jesus Christ, and a burning desire to *act* in decisive ways to uphold honor and decency and that which is lawful and ethical in the governance of our great country. We welcome every single one of you and value your voices and willingness to engage.

And now I'd like to share something deeply personal with you. In those first dizzying weeks, I spent a lot of time on my knees asking God for direction, clarity, and strength. During one of those times, God very clearly let me understand his own vision for Mormon Women for Ethical Government: "I am schooling my daughters," he said.

God is schooling us, sisters. You, me, every last one of us. And not just us, but all his daughters, worldwide. For what purposes, we may only begin to fully understand as we move forward. God is with us. We need to make sure that we are with him.

One of our members, Maren Mecham, captured well the feelings of many of us in those first heady months:

> [MWEG] has excited our inner Joans of Arc; it has made us want to stand for truth (real truth, the pre-"post-truth" kind) and righteousness (the public kind) in a way we hadn't even considered 3 months ago. It has us nearly stumbling over our own eagerness to change the world, rushing in to attend to the daily dumpster fires going on in Washington. It has us anxious to preserve any moral high ground the USA has—until recently—retained and to conserve any democratic virtues which we might still represent in the world. We squeeze our eyes shut against the possibility of losing the noble principles that the American Experiment has validated through its bumpy history. We shut our eyes, but then we take a deep breath, open them again and we go and do things that we've never done before because the stakes are very high.

Our Four Core Attributes:
Faithful. Nonpartisan. Peaceful. Proactive.

Mormon Women for Ethical Government is defined by four core attributes.

Faithful

As our disclaimer states, "Mormon Women for Ethical Government is a private organization and is not affiliated with The Church of Jesus Christ of Latter-day Saints. We do, however, fully sustain, honor, and support the Church's doctrines and leaders."

Members of Mormon Women for Ethical Government are faithful. We believe in, exercise faith in, and seek to reflect in our own lives every facet of Jesus Christ's example.

Nonpartisan

Mormon Women for Ethical Government is a nonpartisan, nonprofit organization. We are not tied to any party or political ideology. Our members come from all across the political spectrum. It doesn't matter much to us if someone is left-leaning, right-leaning, or upside down. We are not defined by labels, but rather by our commitment to ethics.

Peaceful

We believe that as disciples of Christ, we are all called to be peacemakers. We are firmly committed to civility and to treating all human beings, even those with whom we disagree, with respect and deep kindness. We choose to live by our Six Principles of Peacemaking.[a]

Proactive

Mormon Women for Ethical Government was not set up simply as a discussion group, but rather as a "take action" group. Our purpose is not to rant or endlessly vociferate; it is, rather, to take effective action. We recognize that a certain amount of careful discussion must precede any action, but at MWEG we don't just talk the talk, we walk the walk.

---

a. See section IV, "Six Principles of Peacemaking."

IV

Six Principles of Peacemaking

And lift up an ensign of peace,
and make a proclamation of peace
unto the ends of the earth.
D&C 105:39

From the beginning, MWEG adopted as its guide the six principles of nonviolence as practiced by Mohandas K. Gandhi and Dr. Martin Luther King, Jr. and as embodied in the life of Jesus Christ. These principles of nonviolence have a long and storied history. Martin Luther King, Jr. adapted the ideas of Gandhi, who had combined age-old Hindu philosophies with the ideas of Henry David Thoreau, who had been greatly influenced by the ideas of Johann Wolfgang von Goethe, Immanuel Kant, Georg Wilhelm Friedrich Hegel, and others. After much thought and prayer, we chose to adapt these principles for our own purposes and give them our unique MWEG spin.

1st Principle of Peacemaking
Peacemaking is proactive and courageous

We are all called to be peacemakers. We acquire the necessary courage and confidence for this work by filling our hearts and minds with pure knowledge, charity, and virtue.

Matthew 5:9 and D&C 121:42, 45

2nd Principle of Peacemaking
Peacemaking seeks to unify instead of divide

We believe that only kindness, empathy, and pure love can adequately enlarge our souls, strip us of hypocrisy, and help us become reconciled to Jesus Christ and to one another.

Ephesians 2:14, 19 and D&C 121:42

3rd Principle of Peacemaking
Peacemaking demands great tolerance for people and none for injustice

We believe we are all daughters and sons of God and are, therefore, sisters and brothers. As such, we try to possess charity for all and do not wish ill on each other. However, we boldly reject and oppose any attempt to use power or authority for the purposes of self-interest, justification of evil, or exercising unrighteous dominion or compulsion over others. We seek to dismantle all such corruption and the injustices which it perpetuates.

Psalms 82:6 and D&C 121:37

4th Principle of Peacemaking
Peacemaking views human suffering as sacred

We believe it is our Christian duty to alleviate human suffering wherever possible. For those to whom we cannot provide relief, we bear witness to their suffering, mourn with them in solidarity, and persistently shine a light on the causes of that suffering.

2 Corinthians 1:3–5 and Mosiah 18:8–9

5th Principle of Peacemaking
Peacemaking chooses love instead of hate

We believe that love is the most powerful force in the universe and that any sound relations can be maintained only through persuasion, patience, gentleness, meekness, and love unfeigned, and that through this love, the hearts of all people may be knit together.

1 Corinthians 13:4–8, Mosiah 18:21, and D&C 121:41

6th Principle of Peacemaking
Peacemaking believes that ultimate peace is not only possible, but sure

We believe that, through Christ who overcame all, we can have the hope of peace in this life, regardless of our circumstances, and the promise of everlasting peace when Christ comes again to reign forever as the Prince of Peace.

John 16:33 and D&C 59:23

The MWEG Tree:
Organizational Structure & Philosophy

Our organizational structure and philosophy is best described in a group post from June 6, 2017, by Sharlee Mullins Glenn:

> As we've continued to evolve at MWEG, we've spent a lot of time thinking, praying, and talking about how we might best structure our organization. We even consulted with a number of experts in the fields of business management and organizational behavior. But all the talk of hierarchy, top-to-bottom management, etc. just didn't feel right.
>
> One day I took a brisk early morning walk. Winter had turned to spring/summer without me really even noticing. (Hmmm. Wonder what has kept me so preoccupied since, oh, say, January 26th!) I took particular

notice of the trees. Glorious trees—birches, maples, aspens, oaks—rising up from the nourishing ground toward the sun. Roots, trunks, branches, leaves. And it hit me. MWEG is like a tree—beautiful, organic, synergistic, cooperative.

This feels right—MWEG as a tree. No top-down power structure, but a living, breathing organism, rooted in and nourished by the rich, loamy soil of God/the gospel and striving toward and enlivened by the sun/the Son.

It's not a perfect analogy (and like most analogies, it will break down at some point if pushed too far), but it's a useful visual for us, I think.

So, this is how we have re-envisioned MWEG's structure: Our roots, guarded by the founders, are MWEG's Four Core Attributes. The strong, sturdy trunk, overseen by managing director(s), holds our internal support teams. The limbs, cared for by senior directors, embody the broad arms of our mission: to encircle, educate, empower, and engage. Chapters and committees form the branches, and each individual member is a leaf, gathering light and producing life-sustaining oxygen.

The MWEG Tree

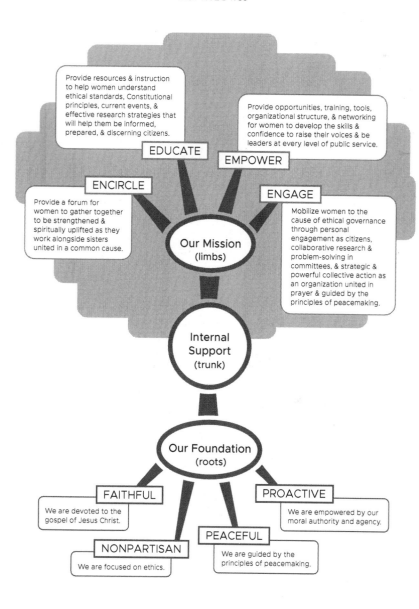

Provide resources & instruction to help women understand ethical standards, Constitutional principles, current events, & effective research strategies that will help them be informed, prepared, & discerning citizens.

EDUCATE

Provide opportunities, training, tools, organizational structure, & networking for women to develop the skills & confidence to raise their voices & be leaders at every level of public service.

EMPOWER

ENCIRCLE

Provide a forum for women to gather together to be strengthened & spiritually uplifted as they work alongside sisters united in a common cause.

ENGAGE

Our Mission (limbs)

Mobilize women to the cause of ethical governance through personal engagement as citizens, collaborative research & problem-solving in committees, & strategic & powerful collective action as an organization united in prayer & guided by the principles of peacemaking.

Internal Support (trunk)

Our Foundation (roots)

FAITHFUL

We are devoted to the gospel of Jesus Christ.

PROACTIVE

We are empowered by our moral authority and agency.

NONPARTISAN

We are focused on ethics.

PEACEFUL

We are guided by the principles of peacemaking.

VI

Frequently Asked Questions

What is MWEG?

Mormon Women for Ethical Government (MWEG) is a nonpartisan group dedicated to the ideals of honor, decency, accountability, transparency, and justice in governing. We are at once watchdogs and activists. Our goal is to share information, organize, mobilize, and act with the intent of both impeding unlawful and/or unethical proceedings and promoting positive change.

MWEG is defined by Four Core Attributes: Faithful. Nonpartisan. Peaceful. Proactive.

Who are we?

We are mothers, attorneys, historians, professors, marketing specialists, doctors, authors, chemists, political scientists, artists, data analysts, teachers, designers, managers, psychologists, singers, therapists, medical professionals, journalists, photographers, healthcare workers, physicists, and language translators, among other things. We are women from all over the globe and all over the political spectrum, united in purpose and vision.

How do I join?

The easiest way to join MWEG is to go to our website at MWEG.org and click on the JOIN tab. By entering your information into the form there, you will be added to our private MWEG discussion group as well as to the appropriate state or region chapter.

Can only women join?

For now, yes. At MWEG, we draw on a long tradition of Mormon female activism hearkening back to our stalwart suffragist foremothers, and we believe there is tremendous power in sisterhood. As one of our members put it, "There is no stopping a group of mobilized Mormon women!"

Can only Mormons join?

No! As long as you agree to honor our guiding principles of peacemaking and as long as you don't mind being associated with a group that is called Mormon Women for Ethical Government, we would be delighted to have you! (You do have to be a woman, though.)

Are you affiliated with The Church of Jesus Christ of Latter-day Saints?

Mormon Women for Ethical Government is a private organization and is not affiliated with The Church of Jesus Christ of Latter-day Saints. We do, however, fully sustain, honor, and uphold the Church's doctrines and leaders.

What are your guiding principles?

As stated in our official group description, "Members of this group are firmly committed to civility and respectful discourse and conduct. We pledge to uphold the Six Principles of Peacemaking.[a] We will not engage in name-calling, vitriol, or hate speech of any kind. We will seek to understand all sides of every issue before taking action." We are guided by our Four Core Attributes: Faithful. Nonpartisan. Peaceful. Proactive.[b]

Why such strict guidelines?

If we are to be successful, we must be united, and we cannot be united unless we share the same vision. Our vision includes an absolute commitment to civility and kindness in word and in deed, and a pledge to live by the Six Principles of Peacemaking. We understand that not everyone in the world would agree that this is the best way to stand for truth and justice. Some want to

---

a. See section IV, "Six Principles of Peacemaking."

b. See section III, "Our Four Core Attributes."

rant and rail and throw things. We acknowledge that we sometimes want to do that, too. But we also acknowledge that as disciples of Jesus Christ, we have been called to a higher path, and we are unwavering in our commitment to that path.

What specific issues do you focus on?

We have particular interest in defending and supporting the **basic rights and dignity** of our sisters and brothers throughout the world. We also seek to celebrate kindness, goodness, and justice wherever we see it. We stand in defense of the fundamental values of democracy and constitutional law.

We are a **pro-ethics** group. We refuse to normalize or accept behavior, rhetoric, or policy that disregards constitutional law, the core principles of decency and honor, and basic human rights.

We are also a staunchly **nonpartisan** group. We welcome women of all political persuasions who share our vision and are committed to the ideals of civility, respect, compassion, and love. The dismay we feel over the current state of affairs has little to do with politics. It's not about Democrats vs. Republicans, or liberals vs. conservatives. It's about right vs. wrong.

One of the Six Principles of Peacemaking that serve as guideposts for all we do at MWEG states: "Peacemaking demands great tolerance for people and none for injustice." This is an important distinction. For MWEG members, it's not about whether we are for or against any particular individual; it's about whether or not the actions, orders, policies, appointments, etc. of any of our leaders are ethical. If they are not, we will oppose those things with all the love and ferocity we possess.

VII

Essays on the
Six Principles of Peacemaking

1st Principle of Peacemaking

Peacemaking is proactive and courageous

Linda Hoffman Kimball, co-founder

We are all called to be peacemakers. We acquire
the necessary courage and confidence for this
work by filling our hearts and minds with pure
knowledge, charity, and virtue.

Blessed are the peacemakers: for they shall
be called the children of God.
Matthew 5:9

[K]indness, and pure knowledge . . shall
greatly enlarge the soul without hypocrisy,
and without guile. Let thy bowels also be
full of charity towards all men, and to the
household of faith, and let virtue garnish thy
thoughts unceasingly; then shall thy confidence wax strong in the presence of God;
and the doctrine of the priesthood shall distil
upon thy soul as the dews from heaven.

D&C 121:42, 45

It is daunting to wake up and—seemingly overnight—
find values we cherish threatened, decorum disrupted
by chaos, diplomacy displaced by bullying and power
plays. How can we respond? One first impulse might be
to take up arms against such upheaval. The mortal impulses of "fight or flight" are potent. Thomas Hobbes'
description of life in an armed "civilization" with no
civility is apt: it is "nasty, brutish, and short."[a]

At MWEG we recognize that humans are not merely
mortal beings; we are daughters and sons of God, and
must arm ourselves with the impulses of the divine. As
children of God we acknowledge the truth embedded
in the lyrics of *O Holy Night*: "His law is love and His
gospel is peace."[b]

---

a. https://yalebooksblog.co.uk/2013/04/05/thomas-hobbes-
solitary-poor-nasty-brutish-and-short/

b. John Sullivan Dwight, "O Holy Night," 1855, after Placide
Cappeau, "Minuit, chrétiens," 1847

Don't assume that a life based on love and peace is flaccid and sustained by limp platitudes. The life of faith—particularly when under moral siege—must be muscular, active, educated, and informed. As MWEG co-founder Melissa Dalton-Bradford expressed, "We will not be complicit by being complacent." We are called to have courage and confidence in God as we arm ourselves to wage peace.

Applying "kindness and pure knowledge" toward ethical governance is new to many of us at MWEG. Envisioning ourselves as "watchdogs and activists" may push us way outside our comfort zones. But too much is at stake. "Pure knowledge" requires us not only to seek the Spirit's guidance but to study issues from balanced sources, hone our ability to ask precise questions, and then offer articulate answers. It requires time, travel, commitment, and enormous bravery to offer what we may always see as our "widow's mites" toward these worthy goals. We may feel inadequate to the task.

These words from Marjory Stoneman Douglas—an author and activist born in 1890, and namesake of the school where 17 people were gunned down in February 2018—long ago gave pointers on developing skills in activism that are still applicable:

> Learn to talk clearly and forcefully in pub-
> lic. Speak simply and not too long at a time,
> without over-emotion, always with sound
> preparation and knowledge. Be a nuisance
> where it counts, but don't be a bore at any

time. Do your part to inform and stimulate the public to join your action. Be depressed, discouraged, and disappointed at failure and the disheartening effects of ignorance, greed, corruption and bad politics—but never give up.[a]

At MWEG we work cooperatively, pooling our experience, talents, and collective wisdom, creating an industrious beehive suited to our faithful heritage. Doing this work together "without hypocrisy and without guile" builds spiritual muscles as we face complex and deep-rooted problems. We reap the benefits of a sense of unity and affection for the other women across the globe who advocate with us, even as we recognize our different points of view. Courage and confidence come from unifying in the service of our common causes. Every effort, tiny or great, is based on the same divine impulses. We each do what we can, and God makes it all holy.

We are promised that the most holy powers of the universe will distill upon us in our efforts. We have to remember that if we give rein to despair and panic, *nothing* will be able to distill upon us. We must be peacemakers for our society as well as seekers of internal, godly peace at a spiritually cellular level.

---

a. Judith Nies, *Nine Women: Portraits from the American Radical Tradition*, University of California Press, 2002, p. 284

In a way, we do in fact "take up arms" in this enterprise. We take up our arms and hands to make phone calls or send messages to our members of Congress, expressing our views on significant issues. We take up our arms to carry posters at rallies, advocating for worthy causes. We take up children in our arms and visit the offices of our elected leaders, mentoring our little ones in active civic engagement. We take into our arms the weeping daughter whose mother faces deportation, offering assurance that there are powers beyond the politics of this planet.

MWEG aims to make peacemakers of us all—blessed by God, and filled with charity, confidence, and the courage of our convictions.

2nd Principle of Peacemaking

Peacemaking seeks to unify instead of divide

Diana Bate Hardy, co-founder

We believe that only kindness, empathy, and pure love can adequately enlarge our souls, strip us of hypocrisy, and help us become reconciled to Jesus Christ and to one another.

For he is our peace, who hath made both one, and hath broken down the middle wall of partition between us.

Now therefore [we] are no more strangers and foreigners, but fellow citizens with the saints, and of the household of God.
Ephesians 2:14, 19

[K]indness, and pure knowledge . . shall greatly enlarge the soul without hypocrisy, and without guile.
D&C 121:42

The book of Matthew describes the occasion when Jesus and his disciples return to Capernaum, where those who collect tribute money ask Peter whether Jesus is going to pay. Peter tells them yes, and then goes into the house to get the money. However, Jesus stops him, quizzing Peter on the customary taxation practices of the kings of the earth. Jesus then tells Peter to go fishing, and that he will find a piece of money in the mouth of the first fish he catches sufficient to pay tribute for them both.[a]

Unlike the term used in the passage where Jesus asks the Pharisees whose image is on the coin[b], the Greek word *didrachmon* used in this passage translates to "tribute money" or the half-shekel, otherwise referred to as the "temple tax." We can read more about this religious offering in Exodus, which tells us that everyone older than nineteen was required to be numbered in an annual census and pay half a shekel as an offering unto the Lord:

> The rich shall not give more, and the poor shall not give less than half a shekel, when they give an offering unto the Lord, to make an atonement for your souls. And thou shalt take the atonement money of the children of Israel, and shalt appoint it for the service of the tabernacle of the congregation; that it may be a memorial unto the children

---

a. See Matthew 17:24–27
b. See Matthew 22:15–22

> of Israel before the Lord, to make an atone-
> ment for your souls.[a]

This beautiful practice was to remind the people of Israel that all our souls are bought with a price. It was a great equalizer in that it made no distinctions between rich or poor. Instead, everyone paid the same small price (about $1.05 in today's currency). That money was used for the service of the Tabernacle so that it would stand as a constant reminder of Jesus Christ and the atonement.

Understanding this context helps us understand why Jesus would not pay the tribute. Jesus points out to Peter that the sons of earthly kings are exempt from earthly taxes, implying that as the Son of God, he is exempt from the temple tax. Moreover, by paying the tribute money, Jesus could diminish the power of this symbolic act. Because Christ is to offer his own soul as the Atonement for our souls, for him to pay an additional half-shekel would make a mockery of his supreme sacrifice and deny the truth of his divine identity. However, Jesus recognized that the tax collectors were not prepared to accept this truth, and he also didn't want to offend, so he set up something of an elaborate resolution. Author Richard Tice offers historical context:

> Since the Jews did not have enough of their
> own coins to cover their needs, they accepted
> coins minted in Tyre. The Jews determined

a. Exodus 30:15–16

that the Tyrian didrachma was equal to a half-shekel. It was not a common coin, however, so the stater (two-didrachma coin) was often used to pay the temple tax for two people together. . . . The "piece of money" that the Lord said Peter would find in a fish's mouth is actually a translation of the Greek word *stater*, a coin that could cover the tax for two men.[a]

This solution allowed Jesus to provide a mediator—in this case a fish with no temple tax obligations of its own—to fulfill Peter's obligation in a way that reinforced Jesus Christ's divine mission. Although it wasn't necessary for Jesus to pay the tribute money, he did it as a personal sacrifice to help Peter fulfill his own commitment. All of this was done quietly, as a private matter between Jesus and Peter, demonstrating that Christ cared more about helping Peter learn from the experience than making a public point. That the Savior was able to resolve the matter in such a miraculous way further testifies of his divinity.

What does any of this have to do with peacemaking and unity? In an endeavor such as MWEG's, there are and will be many times when people with deeply held political convictions come to an impasse. In those moments, our inclination nearly always will be to divide ourselves along philosophical or party lines and either

---

a. Richard Tice, "Bekahs, Shekels, and Talents: A Look at Biblical References to Money," *Ensign*, August 1987

fight it out or agree to disagree. But those are worldly solutions, and what we seek here is divine intervention.

We all must work and pray together to discern that miraculous middle path. As we weigh ethical considerations on both sides, we will inevitably find that sometimes they simply cannot be reconciled through compromise. In those moments, we must remind ourselves that it is in the humanly impossible that the full power of the Atonement is made manifest. We can't forget that the Lord called upon Peter's skill and experience as a fisherman to devise his surprising, seemingly impossible solution. Like Peter, we must draw upon our collective talents, skills, expertise and faith to find creative new approaches. In all our efforts, we should continue to look to the ultimate Mediator. We should model his absolute commitment to true principles and his willingness to sacrifice so that others can remain true to theirs as well. We must be gracious and humble. We should try hard not to offend. We all can resist the urge to divide or categorize ourselves, or to focus on keeping score.

Through the power of the Atonement of Jesus Christ, we have the ability and the opportunity to be made "at one" with each other and with God. In the words of Paul to the Ephesians:

> I therefore, the prisoner of the Lord, beseech you that ye walk worthy of the vocation wherewith ye are called, with all lowliness and meekness, with longsuffering, forbearing

one another in love; endeavoring to keep the
unity of the Spirit in the bond of peace.[a]

By consistently working to develop these traits and constantly seeking the guidance of the Spirit, we might even make MWEG into a fish of sorts—one that can offer a common yet miraculous token of creativity and good will that allows conflicted parties to save face, to feel validated, to move forward.

---

a. Ephesians 4:1–3

3rd Principle of Peacemaking

Peacemaking demands great tolerance for people and none for injustice

Erica Eastley, managing director

We believe we are all daughters and sons of God and are, therefore, sisters and brothers. As such, we do not wish ill on each other and try to possess charity for all. However, we boldly reject and oppose any attempt to use power or authority for the purposes of self-interest, justification of evil, or exercising unrighteous dominion or compulsion over others. We seek to dismantle all such corruption and the injustices which it perpetuates.

[A]ll of you are children of the most High.
Psalms 82:6

[H]ave no fellowship with the unfruitful works of darkness, but rather reprove them.
Ephesians 5:11

> [W]hen we undertake to cover our sins, or to
> gratify our pride, our vain ambition, or to ex-
> ercise control or dominion or compulsion upon
> the souls of the children of men, in any degree
> of unrighteousness, behold, the heavens
> withdraw themselves; the Spirit of the Lord is
> grieved; and when it is withdrawn, Amen to
> the priesthood or the authority of that man.
>
> D&C 121:37

One of the many interesting and little-discussed groups in the Bible is the Samaritans. We first encounter them in 2 Kings 17 when the author outlines his view of their false worship. In Ezra 4, we find another negative story that portrays Samaritans as hindering the work of re-building in Jerusalem after their offers to help were rebuffed by Judahite leaders. Derogatory interactions on both sides continued until Jesus' time.

But then, Jesus himself changes the stories. In the familiar parable of the traveler who is robbed and as-saulted, Jesus portrays a Samaritan as a righteous man who helps the traveler after a priest and a Levite walk by without helping. Instead of making the Samaritan the villain of the story, as his audience might have ex-pected, Jesus makes him the hero who generously offers his time and money to save the traveler's life.[a]

---

a. See Luke 10:25–37

Even more surprising is the story in John 4 of the Samaritan woman Jesus meets at the well. She listens to him, believes him, and runs to tell her village to come listen also. As a result of her advocacy, Jesus spends several days teaching the Samaritans. In one of the most profound messages of the New Testament, the people of the village say to the woman, "It is no longer because of what you said that we believe, for we have heard for ourselves, and we know that this is truly the Savior of the world."[a] Jesus Christ, the ultimate peacemaker, has the power to change lives through His own witness.

And what is that witness? Jesus refuses to follow the prevailing conventions regarding Samaritans and encourages others to do the same by speaking of them without prejudice and including their relationships and interactions in his teaching. He does the same for women, tax collectors and others who experience prejudice in his society. But he also strongly condemns those who neglect justice, mercy and faith no matter what their station. In the Doctrine and Covenants, Joseph Smith writes that the Lord's condemnation extends to anyone who acts unjustly, especially toward the disadvantaged:

> [W]hen we undertake to cover our sins, or to gratify our pride, our vain ambition, or to exercise control or dominion or compulsion upon the souls of the children of men, in any degree of unrighteousness, behold, the

---

a. John 4:42

> heavens withdraw themselves; the Spirit of
> the Lord is grieved; and when it is withdrawn,
> Amen to the priesthood or the authority of
> that man.[a]

This is the power of peacemaking, when we see everyone as our sisters and brothers and therefore work to dismantle systems of intolerance and corruption.

Another disparaged group in scripture is the Lamanites. Mormon in particular often writes of the negative qualities the Nephites see in Lamanite culture, such as their "cunning" and "wickedness."[b] Ammon describes the fear and intolerance of the Nephites toward the Lamanites as so great that most would rather fight the Lamanites than allow the sons of Mosiah to preach the gospel to them.[c] Yet when Ammon and his companions do travel to the land of the Lamanites to try to convert them to the truth, they begin to see the Lamanites in a completely different light. Two of the very few women mentioned in the Book of Mormon are vital to the success of their mission, because both women influence many others by demonstrating faith, humility and a willingness to bring their own lives into harmony with God. Thousands of Lamanites are blessed as both they and their Nephite teachers open their hearts to one another and seek to promote peace through the gospel of Jesus Christ.[d]

---

a. D&C 121:37

b. See Mosiah 24:7

c. See Alma 26:23–25

d. See Alma 17–23

When large numbers of these Lamanites, including kings and at least one queen, convert and decide to distinguish themselves from their unconverted brethren by changing their name to the Anti-Nephi-Lehies, they covenant to never fight again and bury their weapons. Over time, as the religious and political differences between them and the Lamanites result in bloodshed and death, the sons of Mosiah realize that the Anti-Nephi-Lehies need to find a new home. But where can they go? The only viable option is within Nephite territory, but the Anti-Nephi-Lehies justly fear that the Nephites won't accept them.

Then, something miraculous happens. The sons of Mosiah apply to the Nephites' chief judge to ask whether the Anti-Nephi-Lehies could be allowed to enter their country, and the judge recommends that the people vote on the issue. Remember, these are the same Nephites who, only a few years earlier, were telling the sons of Mosiah that it would be better to go to war against the Lamanites than to try to preach to them. But the Nephites soften their hearts toward these refugees from Lamanite lands and vote not only to accept the Anti-Nephi-Lehies and give them land to support themselves, but even to provide for their defense so they won't be forced to break their covenant to never fight again.[a] By doing this, they honor the Anti-Nephi-Lehies' promise, which is so reminiscent of the admonition Paul gave to the Ephesians, to "have no

---

a. See Alma 23–27

fellowship with the unfruitful works of darkness, but rather reprove them."[a]

When we forget that "all of [us] are children of the most High,"[b] we may respond to those who differ from us with fear and intolerance. Left unchecked, such corrosive attitudes can lead to unrighteous dominion and injustice. As members of Mormon Women for Ethical Government, we recognize that we must love all our sisters and brothers, and advocate for those whose opportunities to thrive have been unjustly limited. MWEG works to reduce the effects of fear, intolerance and corruption in our society, and to secure the blessings of self-determination for all people. We do this by seeking out and listening to those with different life experiences and by encouraging lawmakers to consider a variety of viewpoints before reaching conclusions.

---

a. Ephesians 5:11
b. Psalms 82:6

4th Principle of Peacemaking

Peacemaking views human suffering as sacred

Emma Petty Addams, managing director

We believe it is our Christian duty to alleviate human suffering wherever possible. For those to whom we cannot provide relief, we bear witness to their suffering, mourn with them in solidarity, and persistently shine a light on the causes of that suffering.

Blessed be God . . . the Father of mercies, and the God of all comfort: who comforteth us in all our tribulation, that we may be able to comfort them which are in any trouble, by the comfort wherewith we ourselves are comforted of God. For as the sufferings of Christ abound in us, so our consolation also aboundeth by Christ.

2 Corinthians 1:3–5

And it came to pass that he said unto them:
Behold, here are the waters of Mormon (for
thus were they called) and now, as ye are de-
sirous to come into the fold of God, and to be
called his people, and are willing to bear one
another's burdens, that they may be light;
Yea, and are willing to mourn with those that
mourn; yea, and comfort those that stand in
need of comfort, and to stand as witnesses
of God at all times and in all things, and in all
places that ye may be in, even until death,
that ye may be redeemed of God, and be
numbered with those of the first resurrection,
that ye may have eternal life.

Mosiah 18:8–9

Suffering is universal but our responses to it are varied. Each of us must grapple with how to react both to our own pain and to the face of another's anguish. How we experience the latter has its roots in how we deal with the former.

Consider the stark example in Alma 62:41 when "many had become hardened because of the exceedingly great length of the war; and many were softened because of their afflictions, insomuch that they did humble themselves before God, even in the depth of humility." We find additional illumination in the words of Martin Luther King, Jr.:

> As my sufferings mounted I soon realized
> that there were two ways that I could respond
> to my situation: either to react with bitterness
> or to seek to transform the suffering into a
> creative force. I decided to follow the latter
> course.[a]

Each of us suffers; therefore we are universally faced with a choice between bitter hardness and the soft humility that can lead us to be a creative force for good. Chances are that we will experiment with a variety of feelings and actions along the spectrum in between. The reality of a mortal life will continue to feed us pain and sorrow, and hopefully we will inch our way toward greater wisdom and tenderness.

In the midst of trying to develop the graciousness to properly cope with our own pain, we must also struggle with our reactions to the suffering of another. The "natural woman" within us might lean toward one or a combination of the following reflexes:

- Assume and look for a reason that this person has caused their own pain (so that we might learn how to avoid a similar predicament for ourselves).
- Look away, because seeing it is too much to bear.

---

a. http://kingencyclopedia.stanford.edu/encyclopedia/
documentsentry/suffering_and_faith/index.html

- Seek a solution that will quickly fix things, but neglect to invite ideas for solutions from the one who is in the midst of it.
- State that nothing can be done because the problem is too complex and entrenched.

As we resist our instincts to place blame, ignore, fix quickly, or give up, a more complex and compassionate path begins to emerge. This path is one marked by covenant-keeping and starts with the promises we make when we "come into the fold of God" at baptism: to be called his people, . . . to bear one another's burdens, . . . to mourn with those that mourn; yea, and comfort those that stand in need of comfort."[a]

Bearing another's burden means being willing to sacrifice and take on some discomfort ourselves. It implies an action: to reach over and take up a portion of the load. This action can take many forms, and may include reaching out to the marginalized, studying, educating others, and trying to effect change within groups and institutions. When done prayerfully, with guidance from those who are most affected, and in the spirit of keeping our covenants, the Lord will both guide and amplify our efforts. He will open doors we cannot unlock on our own, and he will inspire us to do what will have the greatest impact.

The act of mourning in solidarity with another may accompany bearing, or it may occur on its own. At times,

---

a. Mosiah 18:8–9

we might not have the strength to actively bear, but can find a place in our hearts to mourn. We should not underestimate the power of sharing the sacred experience of grieving with another, whether we are beside them physically or symbolically.

Opening our hearts to try to understand the suffering of our fellow children of God means we often will be confronted with an inability to provide relief in the way our heart's desire. A productive path forward then is to search for the causes of their anguish and "persistently shine a light" so that others who are better equipped to help may know how to reach them. In doing so, we are both mourning in solidarity and inspiring others to do likewise.

The process of examining this covenant-keeping path leads us back to where we started. Christ's suffering is sacred whether people accept it or not. However, not all other suffering is sacred on its own, but it is our bearing, mourning, and light-shining that make it so.

5th Principle of Peacemaking

Peacemaking chooses love instead of hate

Diana Bate Hardy, co-founder

We believe that love is the most powerful force in the universe and that any good relations can be maintained only through persuasion, patience, gentleness, meekness, and love unfeigned, and that through this love, the hearts of all people might be knit together.

Charity suffereth long, and is kind; charity envieth not; charity vaunteth not itself, is not puffed up, doth not behave itself unseemly, seeketh not her own, is not easily provoked, thinketh no evil; rejoiceth not in iniquity, but rejoiceth in the truth; beareth all things, believeth all things, hopeth all things, endureth all things. Charity never faileth.

1 Corinthians 13:4–8

And he commanded them that there should
be no contention one with another, but that
they should look forward with one eye, having one faith and one baptism, having their
hearts knit together in unity and in love one
towards another.

Mosiah 18:21

No power or influence can or ought to be
maintained by virtue of the priesthood, only
by persuasion, by long-suffering, by gentleness and meekness, and by love unfeigned.

D&C 121:41

In his sermon on the mount, Jesus taught that the higher law requires us not just to love our neighbors, but also to love our enemies. It is interesting to note that he doesn't tell us not to have enemies, but rather to love the enemies we will undoubtedly encounter. He even describes how an enemy behaves: someone who curses you, hates you, despitefully uses you, and persecutes you. Yet all those behaviors seem to matter only in the context of pointing out our duties to those enemies: love, bless, serve, and pray for them.

As we all know, this is no small task, particularly because it can't be accomplished with a half-hearted effort. It seems clear that Jesus isn't asking us to simply not re-taliate. Instead he is teaching us that we must be willing to suffer the negative and then find within ourselves the ability to transform it into something positive and sincere. As always, Jesus Christ is our model and exemplar.

Consider the story of Malchus, the servant of the high priest. After Judas betrays Jesus with a kiss, Peter impulsively jumps to Jesus' defense by drawing his sword and cutting off Malchus' right ear.[a] Jesus responds by touching his ear and healing him.[b] Then Jesus says to Peter, "Put up again thy sword into his place: for all they that take the sword shall perish with the sword."[c]

As we try to adhere to the principles of peacemaking, we can learn from Jesus' words to Peter: those who live by the sword will die by the sword. It is so easy and natural for us to want to defend ourselves, especially when we are wrongly accused or unfairly judged. Many of us have experienced this impulse even within our discussions at MWEG, and we have seen firsthand that how we respond matters. When we choose to fight fire with fire, we burn the whole house down. Instead, we can try harder to follow Jesus' example and respond with forbearance instead of indignation—not because we want to be martyrs, but as a matter of obedience and self-preservation.

"Judge not, that ye be not judged. For with what judgment ye judge, ye shall be judged: and with what measure ye mete, it shall be measured to you again."[d] Instead of

---

a. John 18:10

b. Luke 22:51

c. Matthew 26:52

d. Matthew 7:1–2

permitting our human nature to make us defensive, we can call upon our divine nature to be gracious, forgiving and loving—even to those who have not in that moment offered the same to us.

Jesus identifies the development of this divine nature within us as one result of following his commandment to love our enemies. He teaches that we love, bless, serve and pray for our enemies so "that ye may be the children of your Father which is in heaven: for he maketh his sun to rise on the evil and on the good, and sendeth rain on the just and on the unjust."[a] Likewise, Jesus atoned for the sins of the evil and the good, the just and the unjust.

If our ultimate goal is to become like God and be called God's children, we must start practicing these principles now. Our divine nature is best expressed by returning love for hate, offering kindness in response to spite, showing compassion when it is least deserved, and granting mercy even before it is sought. This certainly is no easy task but, as Jesus taught, "if ye love them which love you, what reward have ye?"[b] In other words, if we hope to change the world through love, we cannot be content to be merely loving. We must follow the examples of Gandhi, Martin Luther King, Jr. and other transcendent heroes who chose love when hate seemed the only rational response. That kind of love, which requires deep faith in the One who loved and forgave us all, is our best hope for true and lasting peace.

---

[a]. Matthew 5:45
[b]. Matthew 5:46

6th Principle of Peacemaking

Peacemaking believes that ultimate peace is not only possible, but sure

Linda Hoffman Kimball, co-founder

We believe that, through Christ who overcame all, we can have the hope of peace in this life, regardless of our circumstances, and the promise of everlasting peace when Christ comes again to reign forever as the Prince of Peace.

These things I have spoken unto you, that in me ye might have peace. In the world ye shall have tribulation: but be of good cheer; I have overcome the world.

John 16:33

But learn that he who doeth the works of righteousness shall receive his reward, even peace in this world, and eternal life in the world to come.

D&C 59:23

In John 16:33, the Gospel writer starkly juxtaposes the realities of mortal life: "These things I have spoken unto you, that in me ye might have peace. In the world ye shall have tribulation: but be of good cheer; I have overcome the world."

On the one hand there is the exterior and constant assault of conflicts, enmity and rancor in the world around us. On the other there is the quest for inner peace. Life in the "world" will always offer disarray, brutality and discord. Each generation faces its own iterations. Those who seek to ensure "ethical government" as MWEG does will never run out of challenges.

If this is the case, why should we persist? Will we ever be victors?

No, *we* never will be the victors, and that is the essential point. The verse from John is clear. It does not say "*We* have overcome" but clarifies that it is Christ who has overcome. It is only *through* and *in* him that we find peace.

The scripture sets up a drastic contrast. "In the world ye shall have tribulation." This is a given. The scripture asserts that tribulation isn't going anywhere as long as the world exists. And just when we start to grimly grapple with that inevitability, the verse flips the mood entirely with the utterly unexpected call for us to "be of good cheer"!

It is not that Christ has resolved or will resolve every earthly conflict. It is that he has overcome the entire paradigm of conflict itself. He calls each of us to come to him as our Lord and find lasting peace which tribulation cannot affect. Yes, scriptures tell us that eventually he will come to reign as Prince of Peace, but this invitation to come to him promises that the discipline of peace can be ours *now* with the hope and promise of the Christmas message of peace on earth, good will toward all.

Like the frightened sons of Judah, we may cry to God, "We have no might against this great company that cometh against us; neither know we what to do: but our eyes are upon thee."[a] With our eyes constantly on our Savior and our lives guided by his will, we can sense the fulfillment of the promise of D&C 59:23 in this present moment and beyond: "[S]he who doeth the works of righteousness shall receive [her] reward, even peace in this world, and eternal life in the world to come."

---

a. 2 Chronicles 12:20

VIII

MWEG's Message of Peace to the World

Melissa Dalton-Bradford, co-founder

They were wholly preposterous words.

"On earth peace, good will toward men,"[a] sang angels hovering over a land heaving with political and racial tension, ruled by a degenerate despot, choked by Roman oppression, crowded in on all sides by competing foreign powers—a land which in just one generation would collapse under revolt, its temple razed to the ground.

Yet it is precisely into the heart of such a conflict-rife setting that the shimmering, pulsating words "peace" and "good will" spilled down the conduit from God's presence. Like pure water, they gushed into this murky sphere, sending bright, ever-expanding ripples across the

---

a. Luke 2:14

thick Judean night. Peace, proclaimed the angels. Peace on this harsh, hostile earth.

The word "peace" makes us pause, shake our heads. Can reasonable people really believe in, let alone strive for peace? Can we, knowing what we do of human nature and of mankind's history of soaking this earth's crust in fratricidal blood—can we hope for peace?

We at Mormon Women for Ethical Government proclaim without reservation that not only can we hope for peace, but we must. When we kneel before the Prince of Peace, we renew our covenant to hope for peace, to claim and proclaim peace, and to proliferate his peace.

One can hope for his peace only because it is independent of outward circumstances. His peace begins internally, in a heart aligning itself to truth and light, and once cultivated in that heart, extends ever outward to touch and embrace all mankind.

Such was the LDS First Presidency message to the Church in 1936, when members were urged to "manifest brotherly love, first toward one another, then toward all mankind; to seek unity, harmony and peace . . . within the Church, and then, by precept and example, extend these virtues throughout the world."[a]

That plea for peace came at a time of escalating global tumult. The Great Depression was still ravaging the USA; the Spanish Civil War was surging; Stalin was executing

---

a. "Greetings from the First Presidency," *Liahona: The Elders' Journal*, 22 Dec. 1936, p. 315

his own; Mussolini was forging an "axis" alliance with Hitler; and the latter was promoting a devilish political agenda, which became official when he proclaimed himself the head of the German armed forces. This timing means that five short years following that Christmas message, untold numbers who had heard that call to peace would be called to the front lines in one of history's longest and bloodiest conflicts. On the beaches of Normandy, in the rice paddies of Okinawa, and in the jungles of the Philippines, perhaps those soldiers remembered that, despite the weight of their rifles and their mud-sodden camouflage uniforms, their covenant was then as always to manifest brotherly love and seek for peace.

Whether it originates in Pearl Harbor, Korea, Russia, Israel, Palestine, Syria, Libya or Washington D.C.; whether it is due to joblessness, chronic or terminal illness, abuse, abandonment, addiction, the death of our beloved, or the death of our faith; whether it is global or intimate, modern conflict "mocks the song of peace on earth, good will toward men."[a] Yet our gentle God rejoins all of this sharpness with a soft call to partake of his peace.

It is this kind of peace that both opened and closed Christ's mortal mission. In the hours prior to his death, the Savior repeated the peaceful greeting angels had sung at his birth. Before the Roman guards would barter for his last bit of clothing, press thorns into his flesh,

---

a. Henry Wadsworth Longfellow, "I Heard the Bells on Christmas Day," *Hymns of the Church of Jesus Christ of Latter-day Saints*, 1985, no. 214

and hammer iron spikes through his hands and feet, he taught his followers that "peace on earth" would not mean peace in this world, but peace above and beyond it. "Peace I leave with you," he said, "my peace I give you. Not as the world gives give I unto you. Do not let your hearts be troubled and do not be afraid."[a] In the face of all that he knew would surely come of torture, betrayal and blood (his own and his disciples'), "peace" surely seems a wholly preposterous word.

Or a holy, preposterous word. A blessing. One that is always to be shared.

It must also be dared, wrote anti-Nazi dissident Dietrich Bonhoeffer: "Peace means giving oneself completely to God's commandment. . . . Battles are won not with weapons, but with God."[b] Internal battles, Bonhoeffer seems to be saying, are won and peace claimed when we do "the works of righteousness," receiving the reward of "peace in this world, and eternal life in the world to come."[c]

From a modern-day prophet comes wise counsel:

> No man is at peace with himself or his God who is untrue to his better self, who transgresses the law of what is right either in dealing with himself by indulging in passion,

---

a. John 14:27

b. Quoted in Eric Metaxas, *Bonhoeffer: Pastor, Martyr, Prophet, Spy*, Thomas Nelson Publishing, 2010, p. 81

c. D&C 59:23

in appetite, yielding to temptations against his accusing conscience, or in dealing with his fellow men, being untrue to their trust. Peace does not come to the transgressor of law; peace comes by obedience to law, and it is that message which Jesus would have us proclaim among men.[a]

Will mine be the soul into which his sweet serenity enters? Into whose unsuspecting life will I dare to carry his gentle greeting? With which family members, friends or even strangers will I share his gift of peace that "passeth all understanding"?[b] Will we each experience something new about his peace? Will we believe, receive and gift to another that holy, wholly preposterous peace?

a. David O. McKay, Conference Report, Oct. 1938, p. 133

b. Philippians 4:7

IX

Selected Sabbath Devotionals

Vacuum Epiphanies
and the Miraculous Coexistence
of the Decidedly Terrestrial
and the Astonishingly Divine

Sharlee Mullins Glenn, founder

This past week, I had the opportunity to clean the temple. For four hours on Monday morning, I vacuumed and disinfected sealing rooms and one endowment room in the Mt. Timpanogos Temple, just seven minutes from my home in Pleasant Grove, Utah.

I've always loved vacuuming. There's something about the rhythmic back and forth of the motion, the steady whir of the motor, and those lovely lines left in the carpet that bespeak order, cleanliness, and a job well done.

I often have my best thoughts and receive my clearest inspiration while vacuuming. In fact, my husband and kids sometimes ask: "Have you had any vacuum epiphanies lately?" And so, to find myself vacuuming—in the temple!—was pure pleasure. Vacuuming behind the veil in the endowment room was especially transcendent. All that light! All that white! It was almost blinding. The carpet, the walls, the veil itself. At one point, I felt the very clear presence of someone with me. A spiritual being. I was hoping it was the Savior, but it wasn't. It was my mother, who passed away after a brutal battle with breast cancer twenty years ago this coming November. It was both poignant and soothing to feel her there with me, she who first taught me to love both vacuuming and the temple. We spent a sacred few minutes together there, vacuuming, and then it was time for me to clean the altar.

I knelt at that altar, dressed not in the robes of the holy priesthood, but in white scrubs, with white booties over my street shoes. And with a soft white cloth saturated in some kind of disinfectant that smelled appropriately celestial (I'm sure was good for the environment, too), I tenderly wiped down its pearly surfaces. It was a surreal, but holy experience.

Later, as I vacuumed the hallway leading to the sealing office, I looked up and saw a painting of Christ with Martha and Mary (you've all seen it: the same painting that graces the walls of countless Relief Society rooms across the globe) and had this thought: "Usually I come as Mary to the temple, but today I am here as Martha."

But then, almost immediately, another thought came into my mind, but this one was not my own: "How I loved both Mary and Martha."

Our Savior loved both sisters. How it must pain both Christ and his faithful disciple Martha when we reduce her to "the one who was 'careful and troubled about many things'"[a] and focus only on what appears to be an unfavorable comparison with her sister Mary.

We often forget—or overlook—the fact that it was in large measure the fervent, proactive faith of Martha, the do-er, that allowed Christ to bring forth her brother from the tomb.

Remember, it is Martha who runs out to meet Christ, while Mary "sat still in the house."[b]

It is Martha who cries out, "Lord, if thou hadst been here, my brother had not died. But I know, that even now, whatsoever thou wilt ask of God, God will give it thee."[c]

And it is Martha who is one of the first among all mortals (second only after Nathanael) to recognize and declare Christ's divinity: "Yea, Lord: I believe that thou

---

a. Luke 10:41
b. John 11:20
c. John 11:21–22

art the Christ, the Son of God, which should come into the world."[a]

We do a great disservice to both Martha and Mary when we reduce them to stereotypes, when we define them by one moment in time, one story, one act, one phrase.

We are complex beings, all of us: byzantine mixtures of good and bad, strength and weakness, the sublime and the ridiculous, the profane and the holy. Let us keep this in mind as we do our work here at MWEG. Let's look for the pure, the holy, the majestic, and the noble in each other. Whether it be our next-door neighbor whose car sports a "Build the Wall!" bumper sticker but who is always the first to bring warm, nourishing food to anyone in need, or a member of Congress who voted for something we consider immoral but bravely put principles over party on another issue, let us acknowledge the good even as we boldly call out that which is not ethical.

As I finished up my cleaning shift last Monday and put the vacuum back into the cleaning closet, I thought about the fact that these small rooms packed with mops, brooms, dusters and rags, are right there in the temple, unseen behind pristine doors, but side-by-side with the holiest of holy spaces. And I marveled at the mystery of life and the miraculous coexistence of the mundane and the holy, the earthly and the heavenly, the decidedly terrestrial and the astonishingly divine.

---

a. John 11:27

Perfect Love Casteth Out Fear

Diana Bate Hardy, co-founder

A couple of years ago when I was attending a small branch, we had one particular fast and testimony meeting that was even more unconventional than they often were. One sister with some mental illness issues had taken the stand and was about 20 minutes into her very emotional, heartfelt, peppered-with-the-occasional-expletive, public confession. While she continued with heartfelt pleas for love and acceptance, many of us kept looking uncomfortably toward the branch president to see when he might intervene.

Then another sister in the congregation stood and walked to the podium. She gently tapped the sister speaking on the shoulder and proceeded to hug and comfort her at the podium for about three or four minutes while the rest of us watched quietly from our seats. After a few minutes, the second sister quietly walked the first down to her seat and sat there, continuing to embrace and comfort her. A third inspired sister took the stand next and thanked the first sister for sharing her heart with us and then proceeded to give a deeply moving sermon on charity. What began as one of the most uncomfortable sacrament meetings I have ever attended became truly one of the most inspiring and treasured.

This experience has been in my thoughts constantly over the past few days. I find it to be a beautiful parable of how priesthood authority and moral authority work hand in hand. When it became clear that our branch president would not intervene, the sister who did acted on inspiration and moral authority to minister with great charity. Of the experience, she later said, "I just wanted someone to help her, and realized that I fit that description myself." I do not know why our branch president chose not to act in that moment, but I am convinced that there could have been no greater outcome than what did occur—for both the sister at the podium and for the rest of the congregation.

As we continue to pray for guidance in dismantling racism within and outside the Church, I hope we will draw upon both sources of authority. We already put forth a faithful, collective, and ongoing letter-writing campaign to the leadership of the Church, which I believe has and will continue to be answered in miraculous ways. Now we must also prepare ourselves to respond in faith and boldness when the Lord directs us, drawing upon our own moral authority to move forward in comforting, persuading, instructing, correcting, and ministering to our sisters and brothers within our spheres of influence.

As we engage in this important work, we should remember the words of Moroni, who says:

Behold, I speak with boldness, having authority from God; and I fear not what man can do; for perfect love casteth out all fear. And I am filled with charity, which is everlasting love; wherefore, all children are alike unto me; wherefore I love little children with a perfect love; and they are all alike and partakers of salvation. For I know that God is not a partial God, neither a changeable being; but he is unchangeable from all eternity to all eternity."[a]

---

a. Moroni 8:16–18

Emojis, Gandhi and God

Linda Hoffman Kimball, co-founder

It has been another busy week in our country. Town Halls convened—some raucous, some civil. Phones and faxes rang. Citizens wrote, stamped and sent postcards and letters. Grassroots organizations—many with goals overlapping MWEG's—sprang up. Merriam-Webster reminded the country, despite sound bites to the contrary, that the definition of *feminism* is "the belief that men and women should have equal rights and opportunities." Articles and actions collected likes, hearts, wows, as well as weepy and angry faces.

I caught myself after clicking on the angry icon related to some new irksome development. What am I doing with the anger I just admitted to the entire cyber world? Wasn't it Gandhi—one of the leaders after which MWEG models its approach—the one who said, "Anger is the enemy of non-violence"[a]?

On this Sabbath I will seek lessons from anger. Typically, it is a secondary emotion, masking something more primal—like fear, hurt, loss, betrayal. It is a defense

---

[a] https://allauthor.com/quotes/20411/

mechanism like pain that should draw our attention to the root cause, not the quashing of a symptom with shame or denial. In MWEG (and in life in general, for that matter) our hope is to remain "anxiously engaged" in positive ways toward our worthy goals. When every day brings new disturbing headlines, how do we find our way through primal injuries to a place of peace and action?

Again, Gandhi has wise words: "I know, to banish anger altogether from one's breast is a difficult task. It cannot be achieved through pure personal effort. It can be done only by God's grace."[a]

Today I will ask God to help me accept his grace. I will invite his wondrous alchemy to turn the dark feelings that assault my peace into something green and good, sprouting with gratitude and love.

I will examine the deeper injuries: What values I cherish are being threatened? Why does this feel so personal to me? I will acknowledge the anger and reframe it into something positive. Again, Gandhi provides wisdom: "Non-cooperation with evil is as much a duty as is co-operation with good."[b] If I chance to meet a frown, I will turn it into "non-cooperation with evil" and put my

a. "Glorious Thoughts of Gandhi: Being a Treasury of about Ten Thousand Valuable and Inspiring Thoughts of Mahatma Gandhi, Classified Under Four Hundred Subjects." New Book Society of India, 1965

b. Mohandas K. Gandhi, courtroom statement, Ahmadabad, India, 23 Mar. 1922

impulses to good work protecting a value rather than impaling a foe.

I expect this experiment in moving beyond anger into love will take more than one day's meditations. It will, in fact, be a life's work. I'm clear enough about my own inadequacies to be realistic about my expectations. Another Gandhi quote gives satisfying perspective: "Whatever you do will be insignificant, but it is very important that you do it."[a]

As I go through my sabbath I will renew heartfelt covenants, recommit myself to peace and tranquility, and try to be gentle with myself when I fall short of my greatest aspirations. I will also be buoyed and joyful knowing that I am associated with you all. Through the dynamism and vigor of MWEG I believe the truth of this last Gandhi quote: "A small body of determined spirits fired by an unquenchable faith in their mission can alter the course of history."[b]

Carry on in the good work.

---

a. http://www.quotationspage.com/quote/1372.html
b. Mohandas K. Gandhi, *Harijan Journal*, 11-19-1936, pp. 341–2

To Love as the Savior Loves

Sharlee Mullins Glenn, founder

My husband, daughter, and I attended the adult session of our stake conference tonight [June 2017]. Elder R. Scott Runia of the Seventy was there. He brought us greetings from our prophet, President Thomas S. Monson, and shared with us what he characterized, with great emotion, as "probably the last message I will hear directly from his lips." What our prophet said to Elder Runia and the others in attendance at that meeting was this: "We need to prepare the Saints for the Second Coming. We all need to be better. We need to love more as the Savior loves."

Love. That is how, according to the living prophet of God, we need to prepare for the Second Coming—not by frantically stockpiling food and clothing and fuel and then buying guns and ammo to protect it all, not by building bunkers or studying survivalist strategies, not by scouring the scriptures for lists of signs that we then proceed to check off like eager doomsday criers—but by loving more as the Savior loves.

And how does the Savior love? It's easy to answer that question by looking to the New Testament or to those tender and moving chapters in 3rd Nephi. But what about the Savior as the Great Jehovah of the Old Testament? Isn't his love more demanding and capricious, more exacting and inscrutable?

Nephi delighted in the words of Isaiah, and Christ himself commanded the people of the New World to search them, "for great are the words of Isaiah."[a]

What can we learn from Isaiah about the true character of Jehovah/our Savior and how to love as he loves?

Isaiah, the great poet-prophet who was married to a prophetess, has always been my favorite Old Testament writer. Many of my most beloved scriptures come from the book of Isaiah:

- In all their afflictions, he was afflicted, and the angel of his presence saved them: in his love and in his pity he redeemed them; and he bare them and carried them all the days of old.[b]
- . . . yet will I not forget thee. Behold, I have graven thee upon the palms of my hands.[c]
- He hath sent me to bind up the broken-hearted, to proclaim liberty to the captives . . . to appoint unto them that mourn in Zion, to

---

a. 3 Nephi 23:1
b. Isaiah 63:9
c. Isaiah 49:15–16

give unto them beauty for ashes, the oil of joy for mourning.*a*

- Though your sins be as scarlet, they shall be as white as snow.*b*

- . . . and his name shall be called Wonderful, Counsellor, The mighty God, The everlasting Father, The Prince of Peace.*c*

- Therefore with joy shall ye draw water out of the wells of salvation.*d*

- For thou hast been a strength to the poor, a strength to the needy in his distress, a refuge from the storm.*e*

- . . . and the Lord God will wipe away tears from off all faces.*f*

- He shall feed his flock like a shepherd: he shall gather the lambs with his arm, and carry them in his bosom, and shall gently lead those that are with young.*g*

- But they that wait upon the Lord shall renew their strength; they shall mount up with wings as eagles; they shall run, and not be weary; and they shall walk, and not faint.*h*

---

a. Isaiah 61:1, 3
b. Isaiah 1:18
c. Isaiah 9:6
d. Isaiah 12:3
e. Isaiah 25:4
f. Isaiah 25:8
g. Isaiah 40:11
h. Isaiah 40:31

- For I the Lord thy God will hold thy right hand, saying unto thee, Fear not; I will help thee.[a]
- Sing, O heavens; and be joyful, O earth; and break forth into singing, O mountains: for the Lord hath comforted his people, and will have mercy upon his afflicted.[b]
- But now thus saith the Lord that created thee . . . Fear not: for I have redeemed thee. I have called thee by thy name; thou art mine. When thou passeth through the waters, I will be with thee; and through the rivers, they shall not overflow thee; when thou walkest through the fire, thou shalt not be burned; neither shall the flame kindle upon thee. For I am the Lord thy God, the Holy One of Israel, thy Saviour.[c]

These beautiful passages paint a very different picture of Jehovah than we often see in the Old Testament, which can portray Jehovah as vengeful, easily provoked, and inscrutable.

Recently, my husband and I read Isaiah 55 together. We immediately recognized verses 8–9 as an old seminary Scripture Mastery scripture:

> For my thoughts are not your thoughts, neither are your ways my ways, saith the Lord.

---

a. Isaiah 41:13
b. Isaiah 49:13
c. Isaiah 43:1–3

> For as the heavens are higher than the earth,
> so are my ways higher than your ways, and
> my thoughts than your thoughts.

We both always had been taught that this scripture was about the fact that, no matter how hard we try, we can never understand God's mind and actions. As we studied these verses in context, though, they took on an entirely different and much more specific meaning.

A close reading of Isaiah 55 reveals an elegant treatise on God's abundant grace, mercy, and love. *These* are God's ways. And, sadly, historically, they are not the ways of man. As the heavens are higher than the earth, so are God's ways higher than man's, which— too often—are characterized by tribalism, retribution, vengeance, selfishness, and violence. Far from telling us that we can never hope to understand him and, therefore, shouldn't even try, what God actually seems to be doing here is trying to tell us/show us who he is, to reveal to us his true character and nature.

The chapter begins with an open invitation to all to come unto God and receive salvation: "Everyone that thirsteth, come ye to the waters. . . ." And the price is free. "Come ye, buy . . . without money and without price." We then learn, in verse 3, that God wants to make an "everlasting covenant" with us—with all of us, not just David and his seed—and in verse 7, he calls for us to forsake our sins and return unto him, for he will have mercy upon us and will "abundantly pardon." This is followed immediately by those oft misunderstood Scripture Mastery verses:

"For my thoughts are not your thoughts, neither are your ways my ways, saith the Lord."

In other words, unlike us mortals with our vindictiveness and lust for revenge and punishment, God is abundantly forgiving and loving. Unlike humans, who are often retaliatory and stingy, God is merciful and generous. Divine abundance and joy are contrasted here with mortal scarcity and fear. "For ye shall go out with joy, and be led forth with peace," is God's promise to all who come unto him. "Instead of the thorn shall come up the fir tree, and instead of the brier shall come up the myrtle tree."[a]

Joy, peace, abundance, salvation, inclusion, mercy. These are the ways of God. This how the Great Jehovah, our Savior and King, loves. Let us eagerly prepare for his return by learning to love as he does.

Onward!

---

a. Isaiah 55:12–13

Altars, Altar Cloths, and Our Covenant to Mourn

Melissa Dalton-Bradford, co-founder

Draped neatly on nearly every LDS temple altar I have ever seen is a white crocheted covering. I had always assumed that such coverings were a quaint nod to our LDS pioneer heritage, those skilled Irish, Dutch, Welsh and Scandinavian hands that provided delicate handiwork to adorn our earliest temples. It wasn't until loss ripped through me with H-Bomb force that my eyes were opened to see a deeper meaning.

It was a Thursday evening, one week to the hour after the accident that took our eldest son's life, when my husband Randall and I, weak with grief and staggering under the molten lead weight of shock and sorrow, went to the temple so that Randall could serve as proxy for our 18-year-old's posthumous endowment. We happened to be asked to be the witness couple in that session. Freshly amputated as we felt, we scarcely had the energy to kneel, but managed to by bracing ourselves, torsos against and elbows upon that holy, lace-covered altar.

I recall crying quietly, head hung. Dark damp spots—I can see them still—pooled on lace geometry, as I heard the Spirit telling me, "This suffering is a similitude." My heart cramped. "And this," referring to the altar covering I was wetting with the blood of my soul, "is the community of Saints." I focused on that handiwork throughout that evening, seeing it all as if for the first time. And in each of the subsequent temples sessions I've attended in the years since, I have reflected deeply on the meaning of both the covering and the altar.

What do I now see in those soft altars and in those dainty altar cloths? I see these ten hard truths and endless thunderous power:

1. That life is an altar, not a stage, as I had believed before I knew that I had no control over life. That all my efforts to do the right would not and could not protect me from death in all its iterations. That God does not, in the strictest sense, protect us from life, but provides us with exactly enough strength through Christ so that sorrow can be transformed into joy, suffering into strength, death—the greatest evil—into life, and even life eternal.

2. That before anything else—before food storage, white shirts and ties, refrigerator magnets, theme nights and pass-along cards—our Christian covenant is one of connectivity, companionship, co-mourning and compassion. It is about being stitched together in love.

Alma offered this distilled truth at the Waters of Mormon, when he said Christ's disciples live to bear others' burdens, mourn, comfort, and stand in for God in all things, times and places.[a]

3. That any other expression of faith than the self-sacrificial and other-rescuing is parochial and navel-gazing, and lacks the demands that will create of our simple, single threads Zion, and of our threadbare or shot-through selves, gods.

4. That extending our arms to one another knots—or knits—our hearts together, as we read in Mosiah 18:21. This intertwinedness results in a human fabric where each tatted patch represents a tattered and torn some-one who is, through intimate, single stitches, integrated into our community and into a greater, cosmic cloth.

5. That knitting our hearts with one another doesn't require that we be perfectly whole to begin with. In fact, those altar cloths provide an aerial view of all of our broken bodies and punctured spirits reaching outward to be caught, as if with a fine crochet hook or a stretched hand, by the outreach of another broken and punctured spirit.

6. That our brokenness, while making us poorer and more fragile, frayed or shot through,

a. See Mosiah 18:8–9

also provides open spaces where we can be caught by God. Stitched closer to God, we are far richer and exponentially more robust than we had previously been.

7. That such "torn-to-pieces-hood" (William James' translation of the German *Zerissenheit*) is what we came to earth to know. We can, in our experiences with torn-to-pieces-hood, rail and resist, rebel and rage. But we can also recognize that holes, not wholeness, invite holiness. Spaciousness invites the Spirit, and our wounds are healed through the world's and the Savior's woundedness.

8. That altars are mourning benches, and mourning benches are places of reverence. When we seek to meet someone in their grief, we are treading on sacred ground. This call to compassion—to suffering with another— is not a time for perfection, but a moment for authenticity. Any self-consciousness and perfectionist leanings do nothing to help those who grieve. In fact, they impede genuine connection and will leave the grieving more isolated than before.

9. That, according to Alma, we bear burdens first. (Mow the grief-stricken's lawn, wash their car, take their children for three days.) Mourn next. (Jesus wept.) Comfort later. (*Comfort* is derived from *con+fortis*, or "with strength." Bring all your strengths.) And witness of God

(roll out your footnoted sermon) after we have done all of the above and for much longer than we ever imagined necessary.

10. And I have learned that mourning requires silence. The Jews sit seven days of Shiva. We can begin with at least that many days. We need only to show up, show our souls and sit still. Altars are places of listening more than places of preaching. Real listening is more than a polite or professional act: it requires total focus, effort and inspiration. Listening to those who are suffering will teach us all essential lessons in our shared humanity. "Mourners," wrote one theologian, "are aching visionaries."[a] We will do well to listen to their wails.

As Nicholas Wolterstorff, Yale Divinity School theology professor and bereaved father, writes about altars and mourning benches:

> What do you say to someone who is suffering?
>
> Some people are gifted with words of wisdom. For such, one is profoundly grateful. There were many such for us. But not all are gifted that way. Some blurted out strange, inept things. That's OK too. Your words

---

a. Nicholas Wolterstorff, *Lament for a Son*, William B. Eerdmans Publishing Company, January 1, 1987

don't have to be wise. The heart that speaks is heard more than the words spoken. And if you can't think of anything at all to say, just say, "I can't think of anything to say. But I want you to know what we are with you in your grief." Or even, just embrace. Not even the best of words can take away the pain. What words can do is testify that there is more than pain in our journey on earth to a new day. Of those things that are more, the greatest is love. Express your love. How appallingly grim must be death of a child in the absence of love.

But please: Don't say it's not really so bad. Because it is. Death is awful, demonic. If you think your task as comforter is to tell me that really, all things considered, it's not so bad, you do not sit with me in my grief but place yourself off in the distance from me. Over there, you are of no help. What I need to hear from you is that you recognize how painful it is. I need to hear from you that you are with me in my desperation. To comfort me, you have to come close. Come sit [or kneel] beside me on my mourning bench.[a]

---

a. Wolterstorff, p. 34

Compassion and Abundance

Diana Bate Hardy, co-founder

While teaching his disciples and followers, Jesus was asked by one in the company, "Master, speak to my brother, that he divide the inheritance with me." And Jesus responded, "Man, who made me a judge or a divider over you?"[a]

What a beautiful and probably somewhat unexpected response from the Savior! Christ makes it clear that, unlike the wise teachers and leaders of that day, he has no interest whatsoever in worldly versions of adjudication or mediation. In fact, as he often does throughout the scriptures, he rejects outright the notion that we must compete for limited blessings or resources. And by contrast, he implicitly reiterates that his role as Savior and Redeemer endows him with the power to grant to *all* the full blessings of his Father's kingdom.

I believe this principle is taught more fully in the parable of the Prodigal Son just few chapters later.[b] In the parable, the younger of two sons took his inheritance

---

a. Luke 12:13–14
b. See Luke 15:11–32

and wasted it in riotous living until finally, while hungry and eating with the pigs, he "came to himself," concluding that he needed his father's compassion even though he was no longer worthy of it. The father sees him approaching from afar and has compassion; he runs to his son, falling on his neck and kissing him. He then adorns him with beautiful clothing and kills the fatted calf for a celebration of his return.

The elder son, who had remained with his father and served for many years, never transgressing, was angry and would not join the celebration. Finally he admits resentment for never having received the smallest accolade for his long history of faithfulness. His father's response seems a bit more like a lecture than a comfort: "Son, thou art ever with me, and all that I have is thine." But what did the elder son want from his father? Validation? Gratitude? Praise? Fairness? I think what he needed was a hug! He desperately wanted to feel his father's love. But he seems trapped in the same struggle as the man asking for Jesus' help securing his inheritance: an inability to see beyond worldly limitations.

So how do we move beyond that limiting paradigm? I think we must go back to Jesus' own words, "Who made me a judge or a divider over you?" I don't think we were given the parable of the Prodigal Son so we could ourselves engage in hypothetical judging and dividing. I believe the message of the parable is not that we should be like neither son, but rather that we should be like both. If we want God's glory (to be like him), we must obey and work. If we want to feel God's love, we must allow ourselves to need him.

At any given time, one or the other of those desires may be stronger or more motivating. But no matter who we are or where we have been, both God's glory and his love are available to us all. This is the true message of abundance.

The Art of Discernment

Linda Hoffman Kimball, co-founder

I have a tiny (2″ × 3″) painting of Jesus' face on my wall. It's by J. Kirk Richards and is reminiscent of the Shroud of Turin. There are no distinct features—no piercing eyes, no contoured lips that spoke, "Our Father, who art in heaven . . ." or "Blessed are the poor in Spirit . . ." or "It is finished."

I walk past it many times a day. These fleeting, peripheral glimpses linger with me, settle into me, are becoming integrated into my soul. Constant exposure feels like the wisps of a breeze or a hint of a tune. They are gracious nudges toward something too real to be adequately conveyed. There is nothing sternly precise about it. It's an impression, almost a smudge—reminiscent of Ash Wednesday foreheads among other Christians.

I am not comfortable with fastidious certainty. I know my brain's way of second guessing, of stirring up "what ifs." Common Mormon mantras don't work well for me. I can, however, testify of "the truest" things I have known—those bedrock experiences/answers/intuitions that guide and fuel my life. These I trust. These are what keep me in this Christian Mormon place. I am buoyed by these most reliable touchstones. I walk the walk. I'd say I also talk the talk, but my husband reminds me that, because I am a convert with a deep spiritual life long before my Mormon days, I speak Mormon "fluently, but not natively."

With MWEG, I am new to political activism. I just couldn't not do something. (Does that have sufficient negatives to convey my meaning?) Too much is at stake.

I feel a need to marinate myself in the wisdom of the nonviolent principles taught by Martin Luther King, Jr., Gandhi and Jesus (whose teachings I like to think are part of my bloodstream). The overall learning curve is steep, and I am breathless trying to keep on top of the basics. And that's not to mention the complexities of health care, immigration reform, anti-racism and every other category MWEG tries to address. My new knowledge base is broad but not yet deep, sketchy but not yet not precise.

In the barrage of governmental chaos dished out daily, I often feel overwhelmed, flailing, insecure. The gift I crave most is discernment. Because news, views and ballyhoos are so in flux, I want to hone my ability to sense what is most important, what most needs my attention and action.

One day that could be comparing iterations of congressional bills. A different day that could be building a communal sense of unity and care by high-fiving every sister who posts or comments. Another day that could be talking to a member of Congress about an urgent issue.

The next day it could be taking a break from the hub-bub and going for a quiet walk to regroup and restore.

Without getting centered and attending to my core, I will feel frantic, overwhelmed and confused. When I constantly move too fast, I can no longer hear the whispers of that inner tune or feel the subtle breath of the Spirit.

Another Mormon artist, Minerva Teichert (1888–1976), had a mantra she kept in mind as she created her impressionistic, muscular, vibrant (and I dare say feminist) paintings to illustrate the Book of Mormon: "That he who runs may read."[a]

She knew that many would not have the luxury to stop and ponder the messages inherent in her paintings. She wanted there to be at least a quickly conveyed message, a lure to curiosity, an intimation of the Spirit that could linger in viewers' hearts and minds. She was not concerned that viewers focus on the articulation of a horse's hind leg (although she was uniquely gifted at painting livestock). She wanted them to quickly sense power, dignity, movement, energy and action.

We will continue through the blur and churn of topics, opinions and alternatives. For us all I wish the gift of discernment. Let us develop that art. Let us hone our abilities to perceive the smudges and nudges of the Spirit toward that which is most vital, that "we who run may read."

---

a. http://moa.byu.edu/past-exhibitions-archive/past-exhibitions-1997/minerva-teichert-that-he-who-runs-may-read/

Our Words: A Sacred Firewall

Melissa Dalton-Bradford, co-founder

The April day our family toured Auschwitz and Birkenau, the ice-snow was scratching laterally, metallically, across our faces. We clutched our down-filled coats to our chests, stamped our lined boots, and tugged down on our thermal hats while our guide explained that prisoners dressed in thin muslin shifts and crude wooden clogs, weary from exposure, malnourishment, the 12-hour days of forced heavy labor and perpetual beatings, had stood right where we were standing. And that most of the 1.1 million who died in Auschwitz did so in April. They died—but while dying, they wrote.

They scribbled journal entries, we learned. Or wrote poetry. Or gouged phrases in the walls of their fetid, drafty barracks. Or inked a final dirge on the inside cover of a hidden book. On scraps of paper they penned their last gasping words, words that were scarcely legible when camp liberators found those damp scraps folded and rotting in pockets sodden with the fluids of their author's decomposed flesh.

Words survived, whereas bones fell silent under the benevolent, heavy blanket of Mother Earth.

What do the words of those victims have to do with us here at MWEG? What could be the possible connection between those wretched women and us, whose day-to-day lives cannot begin to touch even the furthest edge of the Holocaust, an "unutterableness" Elie Wiesel called "a universe outside the universe, a creation that exists parallel to creation"?[a] What can we learn from those sisters in muslin shifts and wooden clogs, sisters stripped of everything but their imagination and, if lucky, a crude writing utensil? What would those women tell us about how they cherished, memorized and clung to their words? What did their puny words mean in the face of their gaping fate? What, finally, would they tell us to do with our own words?

This week, we mark both International Holocaust Remembrance Day and the first anniversary of the founding of MWEG. In fact, those two days stand back-to-back on my calendar. Their proximity is significant to me. It ought to be significant to us all.

Part of the significance I'm feeling is that we remember with solemnity from Holocaust history how words can either normalize or expose corruption. How words can blind decent, family-loving folks to the rise of evil. How words can also enlighten. How words, when wielded with precision, can dispel darkness and, like a lightsaber, slash through fakery. How words can debase, elevate,

---

http://billmoyers.com/story/elie-wiesel-on-the-holocaust-victims-and-perpetrators/

divide, unite. How powerful, how hallowed are words. How dangerous. How peaceable.

And we remember from a year ago that it was words that brought MWEG into being. As some of our newer members might not realize, MWEG started as a frustrated cluster of LDS women writers who hoped that our well-honed words might be a means of countering the wild, unprecedented abuse of words we perceived in the highest office of the land. Our plan was simple: we wanted to use words to encourage others to use theirs. We wanted to raise a collective voice for decency, morals, ethics, and our common humanity, against violence and for peace.

A year out, and here we are: women, testing and hopefully proving—with every op-ed and Official Statement, with every measured post and prayerful turn of phrase in the comment thread—that we are indeed worthy of the words God has given us.

At Auschwitz, our family learned that in a building right next to the crematoria, a 20-year-old girl wrote poetry expressing her "abiding commitment to humanism" and "to a moral ideal that rejected all violence and bloodshed." This nameless girl was gassed. The poem outlived its poet, who ended in cinders.

Against such a gutting reality and every other kind of ugliness, moral degradation and villainy, words must be raised like a mighty, white-hot firewall. We must hammer and plaster together—word after word after word after word—a barrier of light, our own inspired wall that will hold against the crush of depravity and falseness we see tumbling avalanche-like over the nation, across the globe.

Our words, to the extent that they echo Christ's words, can bear witness to the truth that, no matter how thick and loud the vain babble of the world becomes, we believe that "in the beginning was the Word."[a] And it is Christ—and none other—who will have the last word.

---

[a] John 1:1

The Vessel

Diana Bate Hardy, co-founder

In preparation for teaching the parable of the ten virgins in a gospel doctrine class a few years ago, I learned a few things about ancient Jewish wedding traditions. The groom became betrothed (or legally married) to the bride first, but then went back to his father's house to prepare a home for the new couple, leaving her to prepare herself and her dowry for their new life together.

This separation generally lasted about a year, but the exact time of the groom's return for the bride was not set. It was customary for him to return in the evening, accompanied by friends who came to witness and celebrate with him. Upon receiving word of his coming, the bride and her friends would gather, waiting outside her home for the rest of the wedding party. The groom would arrive to retrieve the bride, and the whole party would then go with the couple to the wedding celebration and feast.

In the parable,[a] it seems that the ten virgins—the bride's attendants—had received word that the bridegroom

---

a. See Matthew 25:1–13

was coming, so they went as planned to the bride's house to wait for him. Each of them took her lamp, almost certainly trimmed and filled and ready for the bridegroom's grand arrival, for which they had been preparing for many months.

Matthew 25:3–4 tells us that the five wise women "took oil in their vessels with their lamps," while the five foolish ones "took their lamps and took no [presumably extra] oil with them." Then verse 5 seems to tell us that the bridegroom took a lot longer than anyone anticipated, because all ten of the virgins, despite being excited and ready to celebrate, fell asleep waiting for the bridegroom.

Finally at midnight, they heard the long anticipated cry that the Bridegroom was coming and it was time to go meet him. All of the virgins awoke to find that their lamps needed to be trimmed and relit. While the five wise virgins hurriedly refilled and trimmed their lamps, the five foolish virgins begged them to share the extra oil. Unfortunately, it seems that there was not enough extra oil to spare, so although the wise virgins may have wanted to help their sisters, they could only take care of themselves.

Then, while the five foolish virgins rushed away in a futile attempt to find someone selling oil in the middle of the night, the Bridegroom came. The five wise virgins who "were ready went in with him to the marriage: and the door was shut." When the foolish ones returned and begged to be admitted to the wedding celebration, the bridegroom turned them away saying, "I know you not."[a]

For years I thought the moral of this story was that we needed to be always working on accumulating enough oil through personal righteousness to be able to endure until it was our time to meet the Savior. But when I was assigned to teach this parable in gospel doctrine class, I approached it with new eyes. I had accepted a challenge to make sure that every lesson I taught, regardless of the assigned topic, somehow tied back to the Atonement of Jesus Christ.

So I asked myself, "What does this parable teach us about the Atonement of Jesus Christ?" In really pondering that question over the course of a few days, I realized that all of the ten lamps went out while the virgins slept. Then all the virgins arose and trimmed their lamps, meaning they cut and reshaped the wicks to get the lamps burning again, only to find that they were all out of oil. What saved the five wise virgins was not that they had any more oil in their lamps than the five foolish ones; it was that they had brought along a separate vessel, an additional reserve beyond their own—or in other words, the redeeming power of the Atonement of Jesus Christ.

The only real difference between the wise and the foolish virgins was that the foolish ones thought what they had (a lamp full of oil) would be enough. But in reality, none

---

a. Matthew 25:6–12

of us—however wise or foolish—can rely solely on our own lamp of personal righteousness. It's never enough.

So what do we do with that new understanding? It's certainly important for us to continue to "fill our lamps" through consistent, daily acts of personal righteousness. Most likely, the foolish virgins would not have even attempted to meet the bridegroom without the confidence of knowing they were doing their best. However, we can't forget that our own efforts, even if our lamps are overflowing, will get us only part of the way.

Jesus was not kidding when he declared to Thomas and his other apostles, "I am the way, the truth, and the life: no man cometh unto the Father, but by me."[a]

Prophets in all dispensations have taught the same truth. Alma said: "And now, my son, I have told you this that ye may learn wisdom, that ye may learn of me that there is no other way or means whereby man can be saved, only in and through Christ. Behold, he is the life and the light of the world. Behold, he is the word of truth and righteousness."[b]

Furthermore, Christ himself taught the Nephites what they were to do with this understanding: "Therefore, hold up your light that it may shine unto the world. Behold I am the light which ye shall hold up—that which ye have seen me do."[c]

---

a. John 14:6

b. Alma 38:9

c. 3 Nephi 18:24

We can more fully prepare ourselves to meet our Lord and Savior by acknowledging and proclaiming his mission and his works to all those around us. Yes, we should continue to fill our lamps of personal righteousness, a drop at a time. But we best serve ourselves and others by making the Atonement of Jesus Christ a priority in our lives and by teaching others how to do the same: how to access the source of light itself.

This principle applies to everything we do in the Church. We can exhaust ourselves aiming for perfection in any number of commandments—scripture study, temple attendance, magnifying our callings, etc. But at some point after we've done our best, each additional drop just flows over the brim and is wasted. Worse yet, we even still may be failing in our efforts. We will always achieve our best outcomes when we reach beyond our own capacity and go to the source of the light: the Savior himself.

This is what Jesus means when he says, "Come unto me, all ye that labor and are heavy laden, and I will give you rest. Take my yoke upon you, and learn of me; for I am meek and lowly of heart: and ye shall find rest unto your souls. For my yoke is easy, and my burden is light."[a]

This doesn't mean abandon our own loads and do only his work. It means we bring him in to help us pull our ordinary, wearisome loads filled with the trivial challenges of mortality, and learn from him how to better shoulder their weight. Because despite his condescension, he is

a. Matthew 11:28–30

never condescending. His message is one of hope and cheer, for he has overcome it all. His mission is simple. His responsibility is to light the way.

French Fries, Fear and Faith

Linda Hoffman Kimball, co-founder

In early January 2017 I sat across from my 30-year-old son Chase at a table in the cafeteria in Chicago's Art Institute. While he dipped his fries in ketchup and mayonnaise (a taste treat he acquired on his mission to the Netherlands), he reached for my phone.

"Here, Mom. I'm going to put the phone numbers of your state representatives into your phone. Who are they?" he said.

"I have no idea," I answered. I was a new citizen of Utah and really didn't pay attention to such things.

Tapping away at other buttons on my phone, he pulled up a site that tells who your representatives are according to your zip code.

"Here they are!" Chase told me their names. None of them sounded familiar.

"Okay, I'm going to put Senator Mike Lee's name and contact number into your phone. This way you can let him know your opinions on matters."

I harrumphed and grumbled, unwilling to be forced into political activity when I knew nothing about it—other than that the previous November's election had shaken me deeply.

"So, tell me, Mom. What do you want to say to Senator Lee? What are issues that matter to you?" Chase asked, still tapping things into my phone.

"Gosh, I don't know. I haven't studied any issues. I don't know. You really should stop. Give me back my phone." I snatched my phone out of his hands.

We moved onto other topics of conversation (like his impending fatherhood, our travel schedules, his job with the United States Digital Service in D.C., and my various projects). We left the Art Institute, delighted to have overlapped in our travels long enough to enjoy lunch together, and off we went to our different parts of the world.

Shortly thereafter I watched the farewell celebration for the Obamas, knowing that my son was in the vast crowd with my daughter-in-law. I pulled out my phone and sent him a quick message saying something wistful and loving.

Imagine my surprise when within seconds I got a text back with the caller being Senator Mike Lee! What!?

It was *not*, in fact, Senator Mike Lee, but my son Chase, telling me that he was having a melancholy and wonderful time. Short and sweet.

Apparently, whatever he did with my phone at the Art Institute didn't quite work the way he'd hoped. I sorted

that out and restored Chase's name where it belonged—
and never have properly installed Senator Lee's contact
info into my phone.

Flash forward to last night [March 2018]. I had heard
about a new Utah House bill, HB 481, which proposed
to rename one of Utah's loveliest highways after our
current president. I am not in favor of this. I crafted a
three paragraph letter to members of Congress, voicing
my concerns and bringing up economic and international consequences I saw. I checked and rechecked my
message to make sure I hit the right tone between respect for their office and stalwartness in defending my
position. Then I cut and pasted my message, sending it
first to the proposer of the bill, and then to all 74 of his
colleagues.

This morning I discovered a few replies to my comment
that were reassuring to me.

What a distance I have come in just over a year. How
did I move from the technophobic and essentially po-
litically illiterate American I was in early January 2017
(before MWEG was a glimmer in Sharlee Glenn's eye)
into the drafter of opinions and the writer of op-eds?

It is because I have—for the most part anyway—put
my fear behind me for a greater good.

When Joshua was faced with the challenge of overtak-
ing a country and claiming it (a problematic issue of a
different sort I won't get into here), God spoke clearly:
"Have not I commanded thee? Be strong and of a good

courage; be not afraid, neither be thou dismayed: for the LORD thy God is with thee whithersoever thou goest."[a]

Be strong. Be courageous. Don't be afraid. Don't be deterred by how little you think you know. God is with you wherever you go.

And we have President Nelson's shout-out to the sisters during General Conference in October 2015: "We need your strength, your conversion, your conviction, your ability to lead, your wisdom, and your voices."[b]

And then there's this verse: "I can do all things through Christ which strengtheneth me."[c] Letting go of fear. Accepting God's guidance. This is what makes the difference. I could write all those representatives because I exchanged my fear and inability for trust, reliance on God, and courage. It wasn't immediate, but I felt God propelling me. God, of course, is well above party politics. The issue is much larger than that. He cares about my growth, and sometimes he has to goose me into it.

It is the message found in these familiar lyrics: ". . . Fresh courage take. Our God will never us forsake."[d] Onward, sisters. The first step is to lay down fear and move forward in faith knowing that God will guide us.

---

a. Joshua 1:9

b. Russell M. Nelson, "A Plea to My Sisters," *Ensign*, November 2015

c. Philippians 4:13

d. William Clayton, "Come, come, ye Saints," *Hymns of the Church of Jesus Christ of Latter-day Saints*, 1985, no. 30

The Parable of the Plastic Bag
or
The Lord Shall Prepare a Way

Sharlee Mullins Glenn, founder

I want to tell you a story. I call it "The Parable of the Plastic Bag." Technically, it's not a parable, because it's true. But "The True Story of the Plastic Bag" just doesn't have the same ring to it.

So, here's the story. Which really happened, just as I tell it.

One morning several years ago I went for a run. As I ran, I was praying and thinking and sort of spiritually planning my day. I had a lot to get done, and knew I'd have to stick to a very tight schedule. But it all seemed very routine and small-circle-focused (meetings, appointments, kids' school activities, lessons, laundry, meal prep) and I was yearning to do something outside my normal sphere—just something small that would have a positive impact on the larger world. And so I started praying very specifically for that kind of an opportunity, a chance to do some little thing that would make the world a better place.

I came to the corner of 200 South and 1050 East where I needed to turn to get back to my house. 1050 is bordered on the east by a large apple orchard—one of the few remaining in our still pleasant but now nearly grove-less town of Pleasant Grove, Utah. The road there is unimproved (no curb and gutter nor sidewalk), and something about that fact seems to give people license to think they can use it as a garbage dump. The first thing I saw as I rounded the corner was a Big Gulp cup, its lid impaled by a long red straw, which someone had tossed from their car window, and the thought came into my mind: "Here's something you can do. Something for Mother Earth. Pick that up and carry it home to put in your recycling bin."

It was a small thing, but it was something. So I picked it up.

Then I saw an empty Coke can a few feet further on. So I picked that up too. Then a crumpled hamburger wrapper. Then something else, and something else. Soon my hands and arms were full, and I couldn't carry any more. But there, just ahead, was a jettisoned Arby's bag, uneaten french fries spilling from its innards.

I stopped and looked down at it. "I don't have any more hands," I said aloud. "If I had another hand or something to put it in, I'd pick this up too. But I don't."

And then something caught my eye from across the road. There on the other side, nonchalantly sunning itself and fluttering a bit in the morning breeze, was a plastic bag. And not just any old run-of-the-mill plastic bag from Walmart, barely large enough to hold a head of lettuce and a couple of cans of beans. No, this was a full-blown, line-your-kitchen-trash-can-sized bag. A miracle of a plastic bag, large enough to hold everything that was in my arms plus all the other trash I found along that entire stretch of road as I made my way home.

There was nothing particularly earth-shattering about this experience. It was a relatively small, insignificant little miracle in the grand scope of things, but it was a miracle nonetheless. The Lord had heard my heartfelt plea, presented me with an opportunity, and then provided the means for me to accomplish my desire—and his work—despite the meagerness of my own capacity.

And it taught me again an important truth: God will always, *always* prepare a way when our desires are righteous, our motivation pure, our willingness to place our trust in him complete, and our commitment to do all that we can do, despite the obstacles, firm.

I know, as a result of both personal experience and the Spirit's witness, that if we will seek divine help in whatever it is that we are doing—in our families, our callings, our jobs, our activism, the development of our gifts—and if we open ourselves up to receive that help, it will come. The Lord will always provide a way.

And so we must not be afraid. When it seems too hard, too scary, too exposing, too messy, too inconvenient, we must do it anyway if it is right.

The Lord tells us that "[wo]men should be anxiously engaged in a good cause, and do many things of their own free will, and bring to pass much righteousness; for the power is in them."*a*

The power is in you, sisters. Claim that power.

When you don't know what to do next, hit your knees—and then, with God's help, figure it out. Google it, for heaven's sake, if all else fails!

I would love to have a Yankee dime (to use my grandmother's expression) for every time over the past year when I have said to myself, "I have no idea what I'm doing." But then I've gone ahead and done it, because it mattered, and because someone had to do it.

Be bold, sisters. Now is not the time for timidity. Let your fear be swallowed by your compassion, for "perfect love casteth out fear."*b*

We are living in strange times, and we must answer the call of love and become advocates for those who have no voices or whose voices are not heard.

We don't need to wait for someone to tell us what to do or how to do it, "for he [or she] that is compelled in all things, the same is a slothful and not a wise servant."*c*

We have been created to act and not be acted upon. The power is within us. We must claim that power, turn on our lights, lift up our voices.

---

a. D&C 58:27–28

b. 1 John 4:18

c. D&C 58:26

When you answer a call to love, God will be with you. And truly, whom the Lord calls, he qualifies.

Trust this, and go and do.

Onward!

Sharlee Mullins Glenn, *founder*, is a writer, a teacher, a mother, and an accidental activist. She lives in Pleasant Grove, Utah.

Melissa Dalton-Bradford, *co-founder*, is an author, poet, mother of four, and—thanks to 27 years of global nomadism—an intercultural integration consultant.

Linda Hoffman Kimball, *co-founder*, is an artist and writer who claims as her homes her native Illinois, the Boston area where she went to college and became a Mormon, and the mountains of Utah where she now resides.

Diana Bate Hardy, *co-founder*, is an attorney and advocate who is currently taking a break from civil litigation to focus on her young family in Portland, Oregon.

Emma Petty Addams, *managing director*, is a mother, musician, and former contracts negotiator. She spent her youth in Northern California but now lives in Omaha, Nebraska, where she homeschools her three sons and has a thriving piano studio.

Erica Eastley, *managing director*, is a peripatetic introvert who loves to read, cook, and eat anywhere in the world. She currently lives in the Middle East.

Acknowledgments

Many thanks to Nancy Tubbs Harward for copyediting and to Tiffany Tertipes for the cover design.